ISSN | |||||||||||||||||||||||
I0052075

Dediu Newsletter

Author: Michael M. Dediu

Monthly news, reviews, comments and suggestions for a better and wiser world

Vol. 3, Nr. 1 (25), 6 December 2018

DERC Publishing House
Tewksbury (Boston), Massachusetts, U. S. A.
For subscriptions please use the contact form at www.derc.com

Published and printed in the
United States of America
On the Great Seal of the United States are included:
E Pluribus Unum (Out of many, one)
Annuit Coeptis (He has approved of the undertakings)
Novus Ordo Seclorum (New order of the ages)

Dediu, Michael M.

Dediu Newsletter Vol 3, Number 1 (25), 6 December 2018
Monthly reviews, comments and suggestions for a better and
wiser world

ISSN 2475-2061
ISBN 978-1-939757-79-1

Preface

November 2018 was full of events, like the U.S. elections – with some expected changes in the House of Representatives and at the local level, but the budget deficit remains there. The 41st U.S. President, George Herbert Walker Bush, passed away at 94 years 5 months and 18 days.

There are many good news from research in science, medicine, technology, and other areas: a biotech company developed biodegradable antimicrobial paint for ships, Amazon is offering free shipping with no purchase minimum, for the first time, this holiday season, and the Bedford, MA-based company NinePoint received approval from FDA for the AI-based IRIS upgrade for the NvisionVLE Imaging System, which is used in the imaging of esophageal tissue.

In this 1st newsletter of the third volume, the 25th in total, we included the most relevant news, in a balanced approach, usually directly from the source, to help the general public better understand the realities around us. We included also several nice photos - I thank my wife for her photo assistance. Being well and correctly informed is a sine qua non requirement for everybody, in order to make the right decisions for the future.

Enjoy this newsletter and be optimist!

Michael M. Dediu, Ph. D.

Tewksbury (Boston), U. S. A., 6 December 2018

USA, Boston (1630): Charles River Basin (water flowing from left to right, into the Atlantic Ocean (2 km to the east)), with Longfellow Bridge (1900-1906, 539 m) carrying Route 3 and the Red Line metro between Boston (down, Lederman Park (right)) and Cambridge (up, the Massachusetts Institute of Technology is to the left of those tall buildings, including some of them).

Table of Contents

Preface 3

Table of Contents 5

United States of America 7

China, Japan, and neighbors 10

Russia, Switzerland, Eastern Europe 19

United Kingdom, Canada, South America 25

France, Germany, and neighbors 28

India, Pakistan, Australia, and neighbors 33

Italy, Middle East, Africa 38

Medical 45

Mathematics, Science & Artificial Intelligence (AI) 55

General news and issues 60

Humor 64

Universe Axioms 65

Time Axioms 67

Bibliography 68

Paris in 2013: the south-east of la Tour Eiffel (1889, 324 m including the antenna at the top; without the antenna, it is 300 m), seen from Avenue Anatole France in Champ de Mars. It was the tallest manmade structure for 41 years, until the Chrysler Building (319 m) was built in New York in 1930. This Sun-facing side of the tower heats up, and the top moves as much as 18 cm away from the Sun. The Sun also causes the tower to grow about 15 cm. La Tour Eiffel weighs over 10,000 tons, has over 5 billions of lights, 108 stories, with 1,710 steps. The first platform is at 58 m; the 2nd platform is at 115 m, and the third platform is 279 m up.

United States of America

(Population 324.4 M, rank 3, growth 0.7%. Free: 89 of 100).
Reports: The U. S. produce more electronic waste than any other country.

9 November 2018. Reports: American production of oil has reached a new record high of 11.6 M bbl./day.

Reports: More people left California in 2017 than moved there.

15 November 2018. Reports: U.S. state spending topped $2 T for the first time in fiscal 2018, according to the National Association of State Budget Officers, with Medicaid expenditures rising the most, along with a significant increase in transportation spending. Total expenditures grew an estimated 4.8%, compared to 3.8% in fiscal 2017.

Reports: The U.S. Postal Service lost $3.9 B in 2018, even as package deliveries rose 10%. While USPS reported operating revenue of $70.6 B for the fiscal year, its net loss more than tripled from 2017, hurt by rising pay and benefits, and higher transport costs.

Reports: Congress, as a whole, has spent its constituents into an additional $9 trillions in debt in the past eight-and-a-half-years, bringing today's national debt to more than $21.5 trillions.

Reports: The crime total burden in the U.S. is 2.9% of GDP, or roughly $500 billions.
In a recent study, nearly 26 millions of Americans reported holiday packages being stolen from their front porch or doorstep.

27 November 2018. Reports: NASA has successfully touched its InSight lander down on the surface of Mars, marking the first mission to the Red Planet since the previous rover landed in 2012. InSight is scheduled to spend two years drilling into the

surface to study the planet's crust. Lockheed Martin built all three parts of the spacecraft: the cruise stage, the heat-absorbing shell, and the lander.

Reports: Life expectancy for Americans fell again last year, to 78.6 years, and has now lost three-tenths each year since 2014. Economists consider life expectancy to be an important measure of a nation's prosperity, but the 2017 data paints a darker picture of health in the U.S.

30 November 2018. Reports: NASA has named nine U.S. companies, including Lockheed Martin, that will compete for $2.6 B in contracts under the space agency's renewed long-term moon program. "Right now, we're building a space station, we call it 'Gateway,' that's going to be in orbit around the moon. From there we want reusable landers that go back and forth to the surface," said NASA Administrator Jim Bridenstine. "We think we can achieve this in about 10 years... then go on to Mars."

Puerto Rico: (Population 3.6 M, rank 134, decrease 0.1%; an unincorporated territory of the United States, located in the northeast Caribbean Sea, 1,600 km southeast of Miami, Florida.).

United Nations. There are 195 officially recognized countries. Around 44,000 people work for the United Nations. There is a wide range of jobs: Researchers, IT-specialists, lawyers, experts on finance and administration, or translators work at the New York headquarters, at the official locations, or at specialized agencies. More than half of the UN's workforce is employed in the field, in projects of humanitarian aid, or on peace missions.

Boston Harbor (USA, 2014), looking south-east: the port (left) side of Clipper Stad Amsterdam (2000, 76 m x 10.5 m x 4.8 m x 46.5 m) moored at the Marina at Rowes Wharf (1666, 1764, 1987).

China, Japan, and neighbors

China: (Population 1.4 B, rank 1, growth 0.4%. Freedom House reports for 2018: Not Free (15 of 100)). 5 November 2108. Reports: Talking up his commitment to "free trade," President Xi promised to lower import tariffs, reduce investment barriers and broaden market access at the opening speech of the China International Import Expo.

5 November 2018. Xinhua: Chinese President Xi Jinping and his wife Peng Liyuan hosted a banquet on Sunday, 4 Nov, evening in Shanghai to welcome distinguished guests from around the world, who will attend the first China International Import Expo (CIIE) opening Monday, 5 Nov. Xi and Peng took group photos with foreign leaders and their spouses.

On behalf of the Chinese government and the Chinese people, Xi extended a warm welcome to foreign leaders and other guests.

Shanghai is the largest economic center of China and is at the frontier of China's reform and opening-up. It has witnessed the historical course of China's opening-up and cooperation since modern times, and has written a splendid chapter of China's 40 years of reform and opening-up, Xi said.

The CIIE is hosted by China but for the world, Xi said, stressing that it is not an ordinary expo, but a major policy for China to push for a new round of high-level opening-up, and a major measure for China to take the initiative to open its market to the world.

The CIIE will make Shanghai a more shining city, he said.

In the next six days, a total of 172 countries, regions and international organizations from the five continents will showcase their development achievements and international image to the world, he said. More than 3,600 companies from different countries will hold discussions and seek common development with purchasers from China and overseas. Guests will also exchange views about major issues concerning international economy, and trade and global economic governance, Xi said.

This will be a grand event with great expectations, set to create fruitful results for friends from various countries, he said.

"I believe that, with strong supports and joint efforts of all sides, the CIIE will surely become a high-level international expo, which will provide a new platform for deepening international economic and trade cooperation, advancing the joint development of the Belt and Road, and promoting economic globalization, and make greater contribution to boosting the well-being of all people, and building a community with a shared future for humanity," Xi said.

8 November 2018. Xinhua: Chinese President Xi Jinping has called for firm confidence and determination to further reform and opening-up, and accelerated efforts to increase city core competitiveness, to better serve the country's reform and development, during his two-day inspection in Shanghai, which ended Wednesday, 7 Nov. Xi, also general secretary of the Communist Party of China (CPC) Central Committee and chairman of the Central Military Commission, stressed upholding and taking the Thought on Socialism with Chinese Characteristics for a New Era as a guide, and resolutely implementing decisions and plans of the CPC Central Committee.

Xi made the trip after inaugurating the first China International Import Expo in Shanghai. During the trip, Xi visited places including local enterprises and communities, where he learned about the economy, sci-tech innovation and urban management.

Located in Lujiazui, the 632-meter Shanghai Tower is the tallest building in China and the second-tallest in the world. It was Xi himself who approved the design of the building in 2007, and pushed for its construction when he was working in Shanghai.

On Tuesday, 6 Nov, morning, Xi arrived at a Party service center on the 22nd floor of the tower, where he talked with Party members working at the Lujiazui Finance and Trade Zone.

He said the goal of setting up Party organizations in various kinds of enterprises is to provide Party members with services while uniting them to abide by the law, as well as company regulations.

Xi then went up to the observation deck on the 119th floor of the tower, to view the city's skyline.

After viewing a gallery representing the past and the present of the city, Xi said Shanghai is a good example of the tremendous changes that have taken place in China since the reform and opening-up.

Highlighting Shanghai as China's economic hub, and the forefront of the Yangtze River Delta area, Xi said continued efforts must be made to increase the city's core and international competitiveness.

Afterwards, Xi visited a community center in Shanghai's Hongkou district, and inspected the center's service counters, a nursery for the elderly, and a workstation for Party building.

As Chinese society ages, "it is our common wish that elderly people lead a happy, healthy and long life," Xi said, stressing the need to implement well elderly care policies to benefit more people.

Xi also stressed that waste-sorting is a new fashion and Shanghai should make sure garbage management is done well.

He visited the urban management center of Pudong New Area on Tuesday afternoon and expressed hopes for Shanghai to continue exploring a new path of mega-city management with Chinese characteristics. A first-class city must have first-class management, and efforts should be made to ensure scientific, precise and intelligent urban management, Xi said.

When visiting Yangshan Port, Xi said the construction and operation of the port have both created better conditions for Shanghai to open wider to the outside world, and accelerate the construction of an international shipping center, and a pilot free trade zone.

Xi also visited the Zhangjiang science city, where he stressed that the impact of science and technology on a country's future, and the people's wellbeing, has never been as profound as today.

Xi urged efforts to strengthen basic research and application, pay attention to the role played by enterprises, enhance intellectual property protection, value innovative talent, and foster and strengthen new industries and innovation-driven enterprises.

He also called for pushing forward the building of a comprehensive national sci-tech innovation center in Zhangjiang with international vision and standards, aiming at building a cluster of globally-advanced labs, research institutions and research-oriented universities. On Wednesday afternoon, Xi heard a report on the work of the Shanghai Municipal Committee of the CPC, and the Shanghai Municipal Government. He recognized all the work done by the local authorities, and said he hopes that Shanghai will continue to be a pioneer in the country's reform and opening-up, as well as its innovation-driven development.

Xi stressed that China is still in a period of historic opportunity, with a bright future, but tough challenges ahead. As long as China maintains its strategic resolve, and focuses its attention on its own things, the country is set to meet its targets, he said.

Shanghai should develop itself, while serving the whole country, as it occupies an important position in the overall work of the Party and the state, Xi said. Xi ordered Shanghai to better serve the country's overall reform and development. Shanghai should properly fulfill the country's three new major tasks: expanding the Shanghai Pilot Free Trade Zone, launching a science and technology innovation board on the Shanghai Stock Exchange, and experimenting with a registration system for listed companies. Shanghai should exert all efforts to serve the Belt and Road Initiative, the Yangtze River economic belt, and play a leading role in promoting higher quality growth and integration of the Yangtze River Delta, to ensure it becomes the country's strong and robust growth pillar, Xi said.

Xi called on Shanghai to improve economic productivity, optimize the allocation of global resources and achieve major breakthroughs in key technology fields, to make innovation a strong momentum for high quality development. Xi also urged for pushing forward reforms in key areas, and deepening capital market reform, to attract and nurture more home-grown tech firms. Shanghai should build a world-class business environment, promote all-round and high-level opening-up, to lay a solid foundation for long-term development, take a lead in supporting private businesses, and build for them a good institutional environment.

Xi also called for the enhancement of innovation in social governance, to address major public concerns including employment, education, healthcare and elderly care. The quality of basic public services must be raised to ensure a stronger sense of fulfillment, happiness and security among Chinese people, he said.

Party building was also highlighted by Xi, who called for imposing strict governance over the CPC, prioritizing political performance, enhancing the study of the Thought on Socialism with Chinese Characteristics for a New Era, nurturing and inviting competent professionals, strengthening primary-level party organizations, and emphasizing ideological work. During his inspection, Xi also met with senior military officers stationed in Shanghai, and extended greetings to all the soldiers there.

9 November 2018. Reports: China reveals prototype configuration of jam-resistant and counter-stealth quantum radar.

Reports: China's rampant intellectual property theft was long overlooked by the U.S.

15 November 2018. Vladimir Putin met with Premier of the State Council of the People's Republic of China, Li Keqiang, on the sidelines of the East Asia Summit in Singapore.

15 November 2018. Xinhua: Xi Jinping, general secretary of the Central Committee of the Communist Party of China (CPC), presided over the fifth meeting of the central committee for deepening overall reform Wednesday, 14 Nov.

Xi, also Chinese president, chairman of the Central Military Commission, and head of the central committee for deepening overall reform, called for "holding high the banner of reform and opening-up and achieving the overall goal in improving and developing the system of socialism with Chinese characteristics, and modernizing China's system and capacity for governance."

He also urged more efforts to keep advancing the reform and opening-up in the new era.

Wang Huning and Han Zheng, both members of the Standing Committee of the Political Bureau of the CPC Central Committee, and deputy heads of the reform committee, attended the meeting.

The meeting reviewed and approved a series of official documents:

-- a plan to implement an innovation-driven growth strategy in Hainan Province;

-- a plan to develop Hainan into an international tourism and consumption center;

-- a plan to implement fiscal and taxation policies to support Hainan in deepening reform and opening-up;

-- a regulation on the management of the fiscal subsidy fund to support Hainan in deepening reform and opening-up;

-- a plan to adjust policies on duty-free shopping for tourists leaving Hainan;

-- a plan to accelerate the improvement of the reform on the exit mechanism of market entities;

-- a plan to deepen the reform on the government procurement mechanism;

-- a plan to implement the reform on vocational education;

-- a guideline on enhancing the development of county-level media convergence centers;

-- a guideline on deepening reform for fostering world-class science journals;

-- a guideline on integrating law enforcement and approval services at grassroot levels;

-- a guideline on enhancing and improving the publishing sector;

-- a plan to pilot collective medicine procurement;

-- a guideline on improving administrative law enforcement;

-- a document on Beijing's exploration on innovative CPC-led grassroots governance.

The meeting demanded efforts in the celebration of the 40th anniversary of the reform and opening-up and called for "more resolve, courage and intensity in its continuation and deepening."

A statement released after the meeting said achievements and experience accumulated in the past 40 years should be summarized from "a historical, big-picture and strategic perspective," as well as with a problem-oriented approach.

"Since the 18th CPC National Congress, we have not only made many historical achievements, but also created and gathered a lot of fresh experience in reform," the document said.

"To celebrate the 40th anniversary, concrete actions are needed in facilitating reform implementation," said the document, adding that local authorities should take tough action against the practice of "formalities for formalities' sake" and bureaucratism.

It called for strengthened strategic research and judgments on planning both strategic reforms and campaign-level reforms, to unleash domestic demand, boost economic vitality and foster drivers of growth. "Efforts should be made to foster a good social atmosphere for reform and opening-up, and boost people's confidence in reform," it said.

27 November 2018. Reports: Jack Ma, creator of e-commerce giant Alibaba, and China's wealthiest person, has been unmasked by the People's Daily as a member of China's Communist Party. "Political affiliation of any executive does not influence the company's business decision-making process," an Alibaba spokesman told Reuters. Ma has previously described his relationship with the government as: "Love them, but don't marry them."

27 November 2018. Reports: The first genetically modified human babies have been born in China, according to researcher He Jiankui. Healthy twin girls Lulu and Nana were conceived artificially with sperm from their seriously sick dad, but the team

sent in proteins and instructions for a gene surgery via CRISPR/Cas9 to "remove the doorway through which the serious disease enters to infect people." This Chinese researcher who says he created gene-edited babies crossed, what scientists consider, a forbidden line.

28 November 2018. Reports: China is the largest foreign holder of U.S. Treasury debt, with $1.15 T as of Sept. 30.

29 November 2018. Reports: China halts work by team on gene-edited babies.

30 November 2018. Vladimir Putin had a separate meeting, in Argentina, with President of the People's Republic of China, Xi Jinping. The Russian President invited the Chinese leader to visit Russia, and attend the St Petersburg International Economic Forum next year.

Hong Kong. (Population 7.3 M, rank 104, growth 0.8%. Partly Free: 61 of 100).

Macau (Population 622 K, rank 167, growth 1.7 %.)

Taiwan: (Population 23.6 M, rank 56, growth 0.3%. Free, 91 of 100).

Japan (Population 127.5 M, rank 11, decrease 0.2%. Free, 96 of 100). 9 November 2018. Reports: Japan's defense agency is ready to propose unmanned underwater vehicles (UUVs) to monitor East China Sea.

14 November 2018. Vladimir Putin met with Prime Minister of Japan, Shinzo Abe, in Singapore to discuss various aspects of Russian-Japanese cooperation.

28 November 2018. Reports: Unmanned aerial vehicle (UAV) experts at Northrop Grumman Corp. will build three RQ-4 Global Hawk Block 30i long-range surveillance unmanned aerial vehicles (UAVs) for the government of Japan.

1 December 2018. Vladimir Putin met with Prime Minister of Japan, Shinzo Abe, on the sidelines of the G20 summit in Buenos Aires, Argentina.

Afghanistan: (Population 35.5 M, rank 40, growth 2.5%. Not free: 24 of 100).

South Korea: (Population 50.9 M, rank 27, growth 0.4%. Free, 82 of 100). 14 November 2018. Vladimir Putin met in Singapore with President of the Republic of Korea Moon Jae-in.

North Korea: (Population 25.4 M, rank 52, growth 0.5%. Not free: 3 of 100).

Vietnam (Population 95.5 M, rank 15, growth 1%. Not free, 20 of 100). 23 October 2018.

Laos (Population. 6.8 M, rank 106, growth 1.5%. Not free: 12 of 100).

Cambodia (Population 16 M, rank 71, growth 1.5%. Not Free 31 of 100).

Mongolia (Population 3 M, rank 137, growth 1.6%. Free 85 of 100)

Nepal: (Population 29.3 M, rank 48, growth 1.1%. Partly free 52 of 100).

Japan, north-west of the Sendai Station (1887), on Ekimae Dori, the restaurant Rigoletto, named after the famous opera with the same name, by Giuseppe Verdi (1813 – 1901), who wrote 37 operas, Rigoletto being the 17th, with the premiere at Teatro La Fenice, Venezia, on 11 March 1851.

Russia, Switzerland, Eastern Europe

Russia: (Population 143.9 M, rank 9, growth 0%. Not free: 20 of 100). History: 9 November 1818 – birth of Ivan Turgenev (9 Nov 1818, Oryol (325 km southwest of Moscow), Russia – 3 Sep 1883, Bougival (15 km west of Paris, 6 km north of Versailles), France, aged 64.8, Russian novelist, poet, playwright and translator). On 9 Nov, the 200th anniversary his birth was celebrated in Russia, France and other countries.

27 November 2018. Reports: Vladimir Putin has expressed "serious concern" over Ukraine's decision to impose martial law, as the simmering confrontation between Moscow and Kiev threatened to re-spark a regional crisis. Three Ukrainian navy vessels and their crews were seized, and fired on, near Crimea, this weekend, after entering the Kerch strait.

History: Stalin exchanged more than six hundred messages with Allied leaders Churchill and Roosevelt during the Second World War. The messages are ranging from intimate personal greetings to weighty salvos about diplomacy and strategy, and they offer new revelations of the political machinations and human stories behind the Allied triumvirate.

History: The Practical Institute of Technology was founded in St Petersburg on November 28 (December 10), 1828, on the order of Emperor Nicholas I, to train specialists for the developing industries.
Today St Petersburg State Institute of Technology trains specialists in chemistry, chemical technology, biotechnology, nanotechnology, mechanics, information technology, management and economics.

29 November 2018. Reports: Having something, which is only an impossible dream for other countries - a budget surplus - Vladimir Putin said yesterday, 28 Nov, current crude oil prices are fine for Russia.

1 December 2018. Full text of the message of condolences to George W. Bush:
Dear George,
Please accept my deepest condolences over the passing of your father, former US President, George Herbert Walker Bush.

An outstanding politician, he devoted his entire life to serving his country, both as a serviceman during wartime and in high-ranking public posts in peacetime. As US President during one of the most important periods of world history, he showed political wisdom and foresight, and always sought balanced decisions even in the most difficult situations.

George Bush Sr. was well aware of the importance of a constructive dialogue between the two major nuclear powers and took great efforts to strengthen Russian-American relations and cooperation in international security.

I had the good fortune to have met with him several times. I recall with particular warmth him organizing our meeting at your wonderful summer home in Kennebunkport.

My fellow citizens and I will always cherish the memory of George Bush Sr. In this sad time, I would like to pass worlds of heartfelt sympathy and support to all members of your large family. May you have endurance during this time of grievous and tragic loss.

Vladimir Putin

Switzerland: (Population 8.4 M, rank 99, growth 0.9%. Free: 96 of 100). 27 November 2018. Reports: The Swiss government aims to finalize a deal with the EU on a new treaty governing relations in 2019, pushing back the timetable for an accord that both sides had intended to conclude this year. The bloc has been pressing Bern to ease rules that protect high Swiss wages against cross-border competition from skilled labor.

Austria: (Population 8.7 M, rank 98, growth 0.3%. Free: 95 of 100).

Poland: (Population 38.1 M, rank 37, decrease 0.1%. Free: 89 of 100).

Croatia: (Population 4.1 M, rank 129, decrease 0.6%. Free: 87 of 100).

Finland: (Population 5.5 M, rank 116, growth 0.4%. Free: 100 of 100).

Romania (Population: 19.6 M, rank 59, decrease 0.5%. Free: 84 of 100)

Moldova: (Population: 4 M, rank 132, decrease 0.2%. Partly Free: 62 of 100).

Belarus: (Population: 9.4 M, rank 93, decrease 0.1%. Not Free: 20 of 100).

Bulgaria: (Population: 7 M, rank 105, decrease 0.7%. Free: 80 of 100).

Slovenia: (Population: 2 M, rank 148, growth 0.1%. Free: 92 of 100).

Hungary: (Population: 9.7 M, rank 91, decrease 0.3%. Free: 76 of 100)

Ukraine: (Population: 44.2 M, rank 32, decrease 0.5%. Partly free: 61 of 100).

Latvia: (Population: 1.9 M, rank 150, decrease 1.1%. Free: 87 of 100).

Lithuania: (Population: 2.8 M, rank 141, decrease 0.6%. Free: 91 of 100).

Estonia: (Population: 1.3 M, rank 155, decrease 0.2%. Free: 94 of 100).

Serbia: (including Kosovo: Population: 8.7 M, rank 97, decrease 0.3%. Free: 76 of 100).

Kosovo ((Disputed: recognized by 110 countries, and not recognized by Serbia, Russia, and others) Population: 1.8 M, Partly free: 52 of 100).

Turkey: (Population 80.7 M, rank 19, growth 1.2%. Partly free: 38 of 100). 19 November 2018. Vladimir Putin met in Istanbul with President of Turkey, Recep Tayyip Erdogan, following the ceremony marking the completion of TurkStream gas pipeline's offshore section.

28 November 2018. Vladimir Putin had a telephone conversation with President of the Republic of Turkey, Recep Tayyip Erdogan, at Turkey's initiative.

The two presidents continued to exchange views on the situation in Syria. They agreed to intensify joint efforts to implement the memorandum on stabilization in Idlib, which was signed in Sochi on September 17, 2018. They also emphasized the importance of the efforts the Astana process guarantor countries are making to promote the intra-Syrian dialogue.

Vladimir Putin and Recep Tayyip Erdogan discussed Russian-Turkish cooperation in the context of the outcome of their meeting in Istanbul on November 19, 2018.

They also exchanged views on stability and security in the Black Sea region in light of the dangerous incident in the Kerch Strait that was provoked by the Kiev authorities.

1 December 2018. Vladimir Putin met with President of Turkey, Recep Tayyip Erdogan, on the sidelines of the G20 summit in Buenos Aires, Argentina.

Greece: (Population 11.1 M, rank 82, decrease 0.2%. Free: 84 of 100).

Republic of North Macedonia: (Population 2 M, rank 147, growth 0.1%. Partly Free: 57 of 100).

Albania: (Population 2.9 M, rank 139, growth 0.1%. Partly free: 68 of 100).

Cyprus: (Population 1.1 M, rank 159, growth 0.8%. Free: 94 of 100).

Kazakhstan (Population 18.2 M, rank 64, growth 1.2%. Not free: 22 of 100). 8 November 2018. The President of Russia attended the CSTO Collective Security Council meeting in Astana, Kazakhstan. Vladimir Putin, President of Belarus Alexander Lukashenko, President of Kazakhstan Nursultan Nazarbayev,

President of Kyrgyzstan Sooronbay Jeenbekov, President of Tajikistan Emomali Rahmon, Acting Prime Minister of Armenia Nikol Pashinyan and Acting Secretary General of the CSTO Valery Semerikov met in restricted format, followed by expanded talks attended by members of the delegations. During the meeting, the participants exchanged views on the CSTO's work in the context of ensuring international and regional security. They adopted a series of decisions, including a regulation codifying partner and observer status in the Collective Security Treaty Organization.

The President of Russia updated the audience on the strategic stability, and arms control situation, in the context of the unilateral decision of the United States to withdraw from the Treaty on the Elimination of Intermediate-Range and Shorter-Range Missiles; the prospects for possible negotiations with the US side on the INF Treaty; the dialogue of participants of the Astana process, and the so-called Small Group on Syria that began in Istanbul.

9 November 2018. Vladimir Putin has arrived in Petropavlovsk (Kazakhstan), where he will attend the 15th Russia-Kazakhstan Interregional Cooperation Forum.

The forum agenda focuses on new approaches and trends in the development of the two countries' tourism. It has rallied some 500 delegates, including over 250 representatives of Russian ministries and agencies and delegations from 22 Russian regions, which include regional heads and CEOs of large companies.

The previous forum was held in Chelyabinsk in November 2017.

Vladimir Putin and President of Kazakhstan Nursultan Nazarbayev attended an exhibition of promising joint projects, titled New Approaches and Trends in the Development of Tourism in Russia and Kazakhstan.

Meeting with President of Kazakhstan Nursultan Nazarbayev: the two leaders held a one-on-one meeting before the plenary session of the 15th Russia-Kazakhstan Interregional Cooperation Forum.

Armenia: (Population 2.9 M, rank 138, growth 0.2%. Partly free: 45 of 100).

Azerbaijan: (Population 9.8 M, rank 90, growth 1.1%. Not free 14 of 100).

Uzbekistan: (Population 31.9 M, rank 44, growth 1.5%. Not free: 3 of 100).

Kyrgyzstan (Population 6 M, rank 112, growth 1.5%. Partly free, 37 of 100).

Tajikistan: (Population 8.9 M, rank 96, growth 2.1%. Not free, 11 of 100).

Turkmenistan: (Population 5.7 M, rank 113, growth 1.7%. Not free, 4 of 100).

United Kingdom, Canada, South America

United Kingdom: (Population: 66.1 M, rank 21, growth 0.6%. Free: 95 of 100).

Ireland: (Population: 4.7 M, rank 123, growth 0.8%. Free: 96 of 100)

Canada: (Population: 36.6 M, rank 38, growth 0.9%. Free: 99 of 100).

Niagara Falls (8000 BC, the highest flow rate in the world), with the American Falls (left down), the Horseshoe Falls (left up, Canada, 53 m drop, 790 m wide), Niagara Falls city (center, Canada), and an American boat (left) and a Canadian boat (right).

Mexico: (Population: 129.1 M, rank 10, growth 1.3%. Partly Free: 65 of 100).

Chile: (Population: 18 M, rank 65, growth 0.8%. Free 94 of 100).

Colombia: (Population: 49 M, rank 29, growth 0.8%. Partly free 64 of 100).

Argentina: (Population: 44.2 M, rank 31, growth, 1%. Free: 82 of 100). 16 November2018. Reports: Argentina's Senate has approved the government's austere budget proposal for 2019, granting President Macri a legislative victory, and sending a signal to the IMF that his administration is serious about steep spending cuts. Following a plunge in the peso earlier this year, which undermined market confidence, Macri negotiated a $57.1 B bailout from the fund.

30 November2018. Vladimir Putin took part in a meeting of leaders of the BRICS member countries, held on the sidelines of the G20 summit in Argentina.

30 November2018. Vladimir Putin took part in the first working meeting of the heads of delegations of G20 member states, invited states and international organizations; the meeting is held without the participation of the press.

30 November2018. Vladimir Putin and other leaders of the G20 countries continued their work at the summit. The theme of the second meeting is Building Consensus. It is closed to the press. The meeting will continue on the morning of December 1.

Brazil (Population: 209.2 M, rank 6, growth 0.8%. Free, 79 of 100).

Peru: (Population: 32.1 M, rank 5, growth 1.2%. Free: 72 of 100)

Cuba: (Population: 11.4 M, rank 42, growth 0.1%. Not free, 15 of 100). The Kremlin hosted talks between Vladimir Putin and Chairman of the Cuban State Council and the Council of Ministers, Miguel Diaz-Canel Bermudez, who arrived in Russia on an official visit. The agenda included the current state of the Russian-Cuban strategic partnership in various spheres, and prospects for further enhancing it, as well as current international and regional issues.
Following the talks, Vladimir Putin and Miguel Diaz-Canel Bermudez signed a statement on common approaches to international affairs.

Bolivia: (Population: 11 M, rank 83, growth 1.5%. Partly free 68 of 100).

Paraguay: (Population: 6.8 M, rank 107, growth 1.3%. Partly free 64 of 100).

Panama: (Population: 4.1 M, rank 131, growth 1.6%. Free: 83 of 100).

Venezuela: (Population: 32 M, rank 43, growth 1.3%. Not free: 30 of 100).

Guyana: (Population 777K, (rank 165, grows 0.6%). Free: 74 of 100).

Trinidad and Tobago: (Population 1.3 M, (rank 153, grows 0.3%). Free: 81 of 100).

Nicaragua: (Population 6.2 M, (rank 110, grows 1.1%). Partly Free: 47 of 100).

France, Germany, and neighbors

France: (Population 64.9 M, rank 22, growth 0.4%. Free: 90 of 100). 6 November 2018. Reports: France will not rest until its plan for an EU-wide digital tax gets approved before the end of the year, according to the country's finance minister. "This is a clear red line," said Bruno Le Maire. EU governments are still divided over a plan to tax big internet firms like Google, Apple, Facebook and Amazon on their turnover, fearing retaliation from the U.S.

France, Paris, the entrance to Maxim's Restaurant (1893), the most famous restaurant in the world, on Rue Royal, back La Madeleine, 1842.

7 November 2018. Reports: "We have to protect ourselves with respect to China, Russia and even the USA," French President Emmanuel Macron told French radio, calling for the creation of a "true European army." It comes after President Trump pulled out of the 1987 INF Treaty (signed by Reagan and Gorbachev), and demanded more NATO spending from European countries. The EU launched an annual €5.5 B joint defense fund last year, and added

another €13 B in June to support development of new military technology.

11 November 2018. Vladimir Putin attended a commemorative ceremony marking the centenary of Armistice Day. The French capital became the venue for major events marking the end of World War I, which ended on November 11, 1918.

A commemorative ceremony was held at the Arc de Triomphe which was attended by the heads of state of the nations that participated in the war, and heads of some international organizations.

Vladimir Putin, who is in Paris to attend the commemorative events to mark 100 years since the end of WWI, honored Russian soldiers and officers by laying flowers at the Monument to Officers and Soldiers of the Russian Expeditionary Force Who Fought in France in WWI.

Together with other heads of states and governments, Vladimir Putin attended the plenary session of the Paris Peace Forum. The forum is aimed at working out proposals to reduce international tension.

12 November 2018. Reports: The euro is not "a clear alternative" to the dollar thanks to the U.S. currency's international "strengths," French President Emmanuel Macron told CNN. "This is an issue of sovereignty for me. We made a great job during the past years, but it's not yet sufficient... That's why I want us to work very closely with our financial institutions, at the European levels, and with all the partners."

History: Marshal Jean-Baptiste Donatien de Vimeur, comte de Rochambeau (1 July 1725 – 30 May 1807, aged 81.9, French nobleman and general, who played a major role in helping the Thirteen Colonies win independence during the American Revolution) was in Boston. In July 1780, Rochambeau, 55, with the French troop transport "île de France" sailed into Boston Harbor. Thus began 2.5 years of uninterrupted French military presence in Boston, as the city became the most important French base in North America, until Christmas Day 1782, when a fleet under Admiral Louis-Philippe de Rigaud, Marquis de Vaudreuil, 58.1, (28 October 1724 – 14 December 1802, aged 78.1) sailed from Boston for the west Indies, carrying the compte de Rochambeau's, 57.3, infantry.

Reports: Universities have played an important role in Europe in many respects - and they have a major symbolic function. It is not thus by chance that President Macron devoted a part of his speech on the future of Europe, at La Sorbonne, to the project of building European Universities. Prof. Dr. Bertrand Monthubert (Professor of Mathematics, and currently Chair of the Board of Directors of Campus France; he is the Former President of the University Toulouse 3 Paul Sabatier) is involved in this project, its evolution, and the way in which the European Union has been putting knowledge at the heart of its ambitions. The results of this project have not always been at the level of its ambitions.

30 November 2018. Vladimir Putin met with President of the French Republic, Emmanuel Macron, on the sidelines of the G20 Summit in Buenos Aires, Argentina.

Belgium (Population 11.4 M, rank 80, growth 0.6%. Free: 95 of 100)

European Commission, European Union, EU: 28 EU countries: Austria, Belgium, Bulgaria, Croatia, Republic of Cyprus, Czech Republic, Denmark, Estonia, Finland, France, Germany, Greece, Hungary, Ireland, Italy, Latvia, Lithuania, Luxembourg, Malta, Netherlands, Poland, Portugal, Romania, Slovakia, Slovenia, Spain, Sweden and the UK.

15 November 2018. Reports: The EU has vowed to strike back against any U.S. decision to impose tariffs on car imports, stating the retaliatory tariffs would be a "re-balancing list covering a lot of different sectors." After the U.S. imposed duties on steel and aluminum imports earlier this year, the EU retaliated with tariffs on iconic American products like bourbon and motorcycles.

Germany: (Population 82.1 M, rank 16, growth 0.2%. Free: 95 of 100). 14 November 2018. Reports: Germany has been reunified for 27 years now. But the country's division is by no means history yet. Even nearly three decades after reunification, the new states still have more unemployment, and better child-care. There are even differences when it comes to food. If you order a "Jägerschnitzel" in Munich, you will be served something quite different than in Leipzig.

14 November 2018. Reports: Angela Merkel is next to call for the creation of a "real, true" European army, following a similar speech from France's Emmanuel Macron. The German leader said the new force would work in conjunction with NATO, but added that "only a stronger Europe is going to defend Europe

27 November 2018. Vladimir Putin had a telephone conversation with Chancellor of the Federal Republic of Germany Angela Merkel, at the initiative of the Germany side.

The two leaders discussed the dangerous incident that took place in the Sea of Azov – Black Sea area on November 25. Vladimir Putin expressed his views on the provocation, and gross violation of international law by Ukraine's warships, which deliberately disregarded the rules of innocent passage in the territorial sea of the Russian Federation.

Serious concern was expressed over Kiev's decision to put its armed forces on combat alert and impose martial law.

It was pointed out that the Ukrainian authorities bear full responsibility for creating yet another conflict situation and for the attendant risks. All this has been clearly done in the context of the election campaign in Ukraine.

Vladimir Putin expressed the hope that Berlin would use its influence on Kiev to stop it from taking further reckless steps.

It was noted that the service personnel of the Russian Coast Guard were ready to provide additional explanations of the developments in the Kerch Strait.

29 November 2018. Reports: Germany's economy minister has dismissed suggestions that his country's commitment to the Nord Stream 2 pipeline - that will allow Russia to bypass Ukraine in pumping gas to Europe - undermines efforts to de-escalate a crisis between the two neighbors. "Those are two separate questions," Peter Altmaier declared. Russia's state-run Gazprom leads the Nord Stream 2 consortium, which includes Royal Dutch Shell, BASF's Wintershall, Engie, OMV, and Uniper.

1 December 2018. Vladimir Putin met with Federal Chancellor of Germany Angela Merkel on the sidelines of the G20 summit in Buenos Aires, Argentina.

Norway (Population 5.3 M, rank 118, growth 1%. Free: 100 of 100).

Sweden (Population 9.9 M, rank 89, growth 0.7%. Free: 100 of 100).

The Netherlands (Population 17 M, rank 67, growth 0.3%. Free: 99 of 100).

Czech Republic (Population 10.6 M, rank 87, growth 0.1%. Free: 94 of 100).

Denmark (Population 5.7 M, rank 114, growth 0.4%. Free: 97 of 100). Reports: Denmark this year has yet again been ranked, by the European Commission, as the most digital economy and society of all 28 EU member states.

Luxembourg (Population 583 K, rank 169, growth 1.3%. Free: 98 of 100).

Spain: (Population 46.3 M, rank 30, growth 0%. Free: 94 of 100).

Portugal: (Population 10.3 M, rank 88, decrease 0.4%. Free: 97 of 100).

Liechtenstein: (Population: 38,000, rank 215, growth 0.7%, Free: 91 of 100) 17 November 2018. Baron Eduard von Falz-Fein passed away on November 17 in Vaduz, the capital of Liechtenstein. He was 106 years old.

Eduard von Falz-Fein's merits to Russia, a country he left with his parents at the age of six, were recognized with Russian awards. The list of his achievements and deeds includes returning art objects, archival records and various antiquities to Russia, and renovating Russian historical and cultural landmarks and monuments. He has a daughter Ludmila von Falz-Fein.

India, Pakistan, Australia, and neighbors

India (Population: 1.3 B, rank 2nd, growth 1.1%. Free: 77 of 100). 30 November 2018. On the sidelines of the G20 summit in Argentina, Vladimir Putin took part in the Russia–India–China (RIC) meeting with Prime Minister of India Narendra Modi, and President of China, Xi Jinping.

Indonesia: (Population: 263.9 M, rank 4, growth 1.1%. Partly free: 65 of 100). 12 November 2018. A meeting of the Russia-Islamic World Strategic Vision Group is underway on November 12 in Kaspiysk, Daghestan, Russia. It is being attended by government officials, public figures and religious leaders from Russia and 33 other countries, including Egypt, Saudi Arabia, Iran, Turkey, Malaysia, Indonesia, Pakistan, Bangladesh, the United Arab Emirates, Kuwait, and Jordan. The Russia-Islamic World Strategic Vision Group was established in 2006. It is currently chaired by Rustam Minnikhanov, head of the Republic of Tatarstan, Russia.
14 November 2018. Vladimir Putin had a meeting with President of the Republic of Indonesia, Joko Widodo, in Singapore.

Australia: (Population: 24.4 M, rank 53, growth 1.3%. Free: 98 of 100).

New Zealand: (Population 4.7 M, rank 125, growth 1%. Free: 98 of 100).

Pakistan: (Population 212 M, rank 5, growth 2%. Partly free: 43 of 100). 3 November 2018. Xinhua: Chinese President Xi Jinping met with Pakistani Prime Minister, Imran Khan, in Beijing Friday, 2 Nov.
Xi welcomed Khan for paying an official visit to China, and attending the first China International Import Expo.
He hailed the China-Pakistan all-weather strategic cooperative partnership, as a special friendship shaped and developed during a long time of mutual support and close cooperation.

Xi said the bilateral ties always stay vigorous and continue developing regardless of the changes in international situations or the two countries' domestic affairs. "China-Pakistan cooperation not only benefits both peoples but also contributes to regional and world peace, stability and development," Xi said.

Xi appreciated Khan for repeatedly stressing that he would view the relations with China as a political cornerstone in Pakistan's foreign policy, and would unswervingly promote the construction of the China-Pakistan Economic Corridor (CPEC).

Xi said China always views relations with Pakistan as a priority of diplomacy, and supports Pakistan in safeguarding national independence, sovereignty and territorial integrity. He also expressed support for Pakistan's new government in implementing its policies and promoting national development.

"We'd like to work with Pakistan to strengthen the all-weather strategic cooperative partnership and build a closer community with a shared future between the two countries." Xi said the two sides should deepen strategic communication, maintain regular visits and meetings between the two countries' leaders, and enhance experience-sharing in the governance of a country. Proposing closer pragmatic cooperation and promotion in trade and investment, Xi called for consolidating the early results of CPEC and expanding CPEC to areas such as industrial parks and people's livelihood.

He also said the two sides should boost people-to-people exchanges, strengthen anti-terrorism cooperation, and increase coordination and communication on multilateral platforms, such as the United Nations and the Shanghai Cooperation Organization.

Pakistan admires China's development achievements, and hopes to learn from China's experience in development, poverty alleviation and anti-corruption, Khan said.

"Pakistan-China friendship is deeply rooted in the mind of Pakistani people," Khan said, noting that Pakistan is devoted to furthering the relations with China, and the construction of CPEC, so as to benefit the economic and social development of Pakistan.

The Pakistani side is willing to reinforce communication and coordination in multilateral affairs with China, Khan added.

Philippines: (Population 104.9 M, rank 13, growth 1.5%. Partly free 63 of 100).

Singapore: (Population 5.7 M, rank 115, growth 1.5%. Partly free 51 of 100). 12 November 2018. Reports: World leaders are heading to Singapore for the semiannual ASEAN summit, where Chinese Premier Li Keqiang is expected to rally support for the Regional Comprehensive Economic Partnership, a free trade deal that will encompass more than a third of the world's GDP. The pact currently includes 16 countries, including China, India, Japan and South Korea, but not the United States.

13 November 2018. The President of Russia arrived in Singapore on a three-day state visit to attend the Russia – Association of Southeast Asian Nations (ASEAN) summit, and the 13th East Asia Summit. During his stay, Vladimir Putin and President of Singapore Halimah Yacob are to attend the groundbreaking ceremony for a Russian Cultural Centre.

14 November 2018. The President of Russia took part in a plenary meeting of the Russia-ASEAN summit, in Singapore.
The summit participants discussed the deepening of cooperation in trade, investment and humanitarian spheres, the strengthening of ties between the Association of Southeast Asian Nations and the Shanghai Cooperation Organization, as well as current international and regional issues.
ASEAN comprises 10 Southeast Asian countries: Brunei Darussalam, Cambodia, Indonesia, Laos, Malaysia, Myanmar, the Philippines, Singapore, Thailand and Vietnam. Russia became a dialogue partner in July 1996

14 November 2018. The President of Russia met with Prime Minister of the Republic of Singapore, Lee Hsien Loong.

15 November 2018. Vladimir Putin attended the plenary session of the 13th East Asia Summit (EAS). The discussion focused on strengthening regional security, countering terrorism and promoting cooperation in healthcare, high technology and environmental protection. The meeting was closed to the media.
At the East Asia Summit the President of Russia had brief meetings with U.S. Vice President Michael Pence, and Assistant to the US President for National Security Affairs, John Bolton, as well as with Prime Minister of India, Narendra Modi.
The East Asia Summit (EAS) was held in Singapore. The EAS currently comprises 18 countries: 10 ASEAN members (Brunei

Darussalam, Cambodia, Indonesia, Laos, Malaysia, Myanmar, the Philippines, Singapore, Thailand and Vietnam), and eight dialogue partners: Russia (joined the EAS in 2010), the United States, Japan, South Korea, India, China, Australia and New Zealand.

APEC (21 members: Singapore, China, USA, Vietnam, Australia, Japan, Indonesia, Russia, Philippines, Malaysia, Hong Kong, Thailand, Chile, Canada, New Zealand, South Korea, Peru, Mexico, Brunei, Papua New Guinea, Chinese Taipei)

Thailand: (Population 69 M, rank 20, growth 0.3%. Not free 32 of 100). 14 November 2018. The President of Russia met with Prime Minister of the Kingdom of Thailand, Prayut Chan-o-cha, in Singapore.

Myanmar (Burma, Population 53.3 M, rank 26, growth 0.9%. Not free 32 of 100

Bangladesh (Population 164.6 M, rank 8, growth 1.1%. Partly free 47 of 100).

Sri Lanka (Population 20.8 M, rank 58, growth 0.4%. Partly free 56 of 100).

Malaysia (Population 31.6 M, rank 45, growth 1.34%. Partly free 44 of 100). 13 November 2018. Vladimir Putin met with Malaysian Prime Minister, Mahathir Mohamad, as part of his visit to Singapore.

Brunei: (Population 428,000, rank 176, growth 1.3%. Not free 29 of 100).

Vanuatu: (Population 276,000, rank 185, growth 2.2%. Free 80 of 100)

Tonga: (Population 108,000, rank 195, growth 0.8%. Free 74 of 100). 3 November 2018. Xinhua: Chinese President Xi Jinping and Tongan King Tupou VI exchanged congratulatory messages on Friday, 2 Nov, to mark the 20th anniversary of the establishment of diplomatic ties between the two countries.

In his message to King Tupou VI, Xi said that bilateral ties have grown continuously with the expansion of practical cooperation, and people-to-people exchanges over the past two decades.

Xi said that he and King Tupou VI achieved important consensus on promoting bilateral exchanges and cooperation on a wide range of areas, during the king's state visit to China in March this year, which outlined the direction for future bilateral ties. Xi said that he greatly values China-Tonga relations and is willing to make use of the opportunity of the 20th anniversary of diplomatic relations to strengthen exchanges and cooperation, and constantly scale new heights in the relationship, so as to better benefit the two peoples.

In his congratulatory message to Xi, King Tupou VI said high-level exchanges between the two countries are robust, cooperation is expanding, and mutual understanding and friendship between the two peoples are growing. The king also sent his wishes for China's prosperity, and the well-being of the Chinese people.

Papua New Guinea: (Population 8.2 M, rank 101, growth 2.1%, Partly Free 64 of 100). 19 November 2018. Reports: Asia-Pacific leaders failed to agree on a communique at the APEC (21 members: Singapore, China, USA, Vietnam, Australia, Japan, Indonesia, Russia, Philippines, Malaysia, Hong Kong, Thailand, Chile, Canada, New Zealand, South Korea, Peru, Mexico, Brunei, Papua New Guinea, Chinese Taipei) conference in Papua New Guinea for the first time since the gathering began in 1993. Deep divisions between the U.S. and China over trade and investment stymied cooperation, as well as tariffs and the Belt and Road initiative. Another sticking point was whether to mention the World Trade Organization, and its possible reform in the Leaders' Declaration.

Italy, Middle East, Africa

Italy: (Population 59.3 M, rank 23, decrease 0.1%. Free: 89 of 100). History: Research beneath the Basilica di San Giovanni in Laterano (Archbasilica of St. John Lateran, the Pope's official seat, 1 km southeast of the Amphitheatrum Flavium (Colosseum)) has revealed the appearance of world's first cathedral and the transformations that preceded its construction. A team of archaeologists from Newcastle University, UK, the universities of Florence and Amsterdam, and the Vatican Museums, have worked far beneath the streets of Rome to piece together a pivotal moment in the history of the eternal city, supported throughout by the British School at Rome

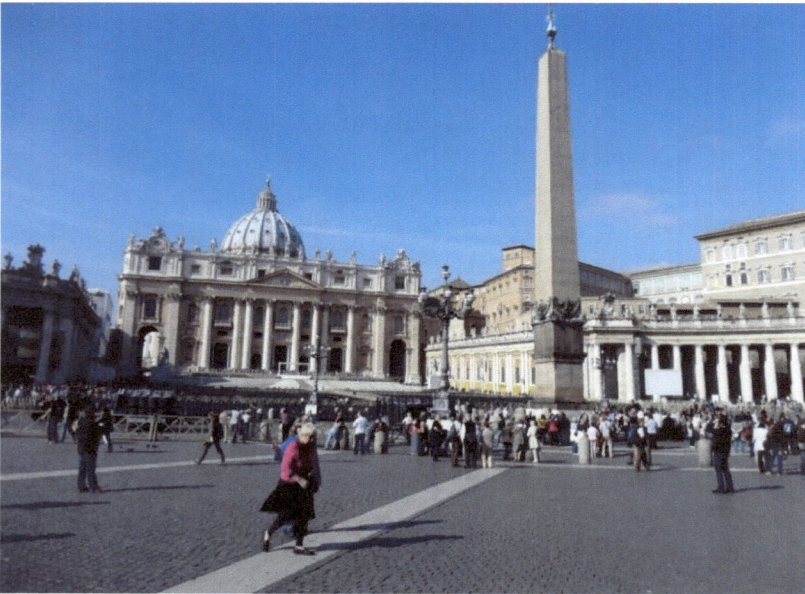

Rome (753 BC), Vatican (1929): Piazza di San Pietro (1656 – 1667, Bernini), with Moderno's façade (115 m wide, 46 m high) of the Basilica di San Pietro (1506 – 1626), and an Egyptian obelisk (1250 BC, 25.5 m, total height 40 m), moved here in 1586.

The church was originally built in 312 by Constantine - the first Roman emperor to convert to Christianity. Positioned on the Caelian Hill, the church would have dominated the Roman skyline at the time. As research reveals, the site had already been in use for centuries. To build his magnificent cathedral, Constantine had swept away the Castra Nova (New Fort), the lavish headquarters of the imperial horse guard, constructed over a century before by the Roman Emperor Septimius Severus (11 April 145 – 4 Feb 211, aged 65.8, Emperor for 18 years: 193 – 211). In much the same way, Severus had previously destroyed the palatial houses of some of Rome's most powerful residents to make way for the horse guards' impressive new home. Working far beneath the modern streets of Rome, the team on the Lateran Project have brought to life the first ever holistic picture of hundreds of years of Roman history by using digital mapping, ground penetrating radar, and 3D visualization techniques. Working with some of the world's leading visualization specialists, the team has reconstructed the splendor of the buildings. It is one of the first projects in the world to have used terrestrial laser-scanning over such a large area, to drive archaeological research. The work has also permitted study of how the different buildings that occupied the site evolved, how different elements relate to one another, and has given a sense of the scale the four-hectare site covers. The work carried out by the Lateran Project is featured in the latest edition of Current World Archaeology. Professor Ian Haynes, Co-Director of the Lateran Project and Professor of Archaeology at Newcastle University, UK, said: "There is a large area of space underneath the Lateran that it is possible to walk or crawl through." "The archaeology is at varying levels below - at the deepest we were 8.5 m below modern ground surface. To access some of the spaces we worked with a group called Roma Sotteranea, who specialize in working on buried sites and use exactly the same equipment and techniques as potholers." The construction of the cathedral was a pivotal moment marking the start of the major Christian buildings that came to define Rome and is a potent symbol of the military making way for religion. In 312 Constantine's army fought the Battle of Milvian Bridge, after which the old Horse Guards base and several nearby buildings were destroyed. The land was given to the Church, and provided the perfect spot for Constantine to set out his new vision for Rome. "The cathedral was rebuilt in the 1650s but there is still original Constantine fabric in the walls, while the original foundations are exposed beneath the church." "There have been various efforts to reconstruct it since then, so we wanted to pull together all of this information to create a digital cathedral that you can walk around." "Working with colleagues at the University of Amsterdam and Newcastle-based visualization specialists, New Visions, we've incorporated information from earlier excavations. We also created a simpler model to test the acoustics, and to try to understand how sounds would have worked in the basilica."

Vatican: (Population 792, rank 233 (last), decrease 1.1%).

San Marino: (Population 33,400, rank 218, growth 0.6%. Free 97 of 100)

Jordan (Population 9.7 M, rank 92, growth 2.6%. Partly free, 37 of 100).

Lebanon: (Population: 6 M, rank 111, growth 1.3%. Partly free: 44 of 100).

United Arab Emirates (UAE) (Population: 9.4 M, rank 94, growth 1.4%. Not free, 20 of 100).

Saudi Arabia (Population 32.9 M, rank 41, growth 2.1%. Not free: 10 of 100). 6 November 2018. Reports: Seeking to diversify his nation's energy mix, Saudi Crown Prince, Mohammed bin Salman, has laid the foundation for the kingdom's first nuclear research reactor, among seven projects launched during a visit to Riyadh's King Abdulaziz City for Science and Technology. The world's top crude exporter hopes to build 16 reactors over the next two decades for $80 B, despite concerns over nuclear proliferation in the Middle East.

1 December 2018. Vladimir Putin met with Crown Prince and Defense Minister of Saudi Arabia, Mohammad bin Salman Al Saud, in Buenos Aires, Argentina.

Yemen (Population 28.2 M, rank 50, growth 2.4%. Not free: 14 of 100).

Iraq (Population 38.2 M, rank 36, growth 2.9%. Not free: 27 of 100).

Iran: (Population 81.1 M, rank 18, growth 1.1%. Not free: 17 of 100. 5 November 2018. Reports: In a meeting with top economic officials, Iranian President Hassan Rouhani said Tehran will "sell its oil and break sanctions" reimposed by the U.S. on its energy and banking sectors. "This is an economic war against Iran, but we are prepared to resist any pressure," he declared. Meanwhile, China said its lawful trade cooperation with Iran should be respected.

Israel: (Population 8.3 M, rank 100, growth 1.6%. Free: 80 of 100).

Palestine: (Population 4.9 M (rank 121, grows 2.7%). Not free: 28 of 100).

Egypt (Population 97.5 M (rank 14, grows 1.9%). Not free, 26 of 100).

League of Arab States (LAS) (22 countries: Algeria, Bahrein, Comoros, Djibouti, Egypt, Iraq, Jordan, Kuwait, Lebanon, Libya, Mauritania, Morocco, Oman, Palestine, Qatar, Saudi Arabia, Somalia, Sudan, Syria, Tunisia, United Arab Emirates and Yemen).

Qatar: (Population 2.6 M (rank 142, grows 2.7%). Not free: 26 of 100).

Kuwait: (Population 4.1 M (rank 130, grows 2.1%). Partly free: 36 of 100). 7 November 2018. Reports: Kuwait Airways orders eight widebody Airbus A330-800 commercial aviation aircraft.

Oman: (Population 4.6 M (rank 127, grows 4.8%). Not free: 25 of 100)

Bahrain: (Population 1.5 M (rank 152, grows 4.7%). Not free: 12 of 100).

Syria: (Population 18.2 M (rank 63, decrease 0.9%). Not free: 0 of 100).

Kenya: (Population 49.7 M (rank 28, growth 2.6%. Partly free, 51 of 100).

Libya: (Population 6.3 M, rank 109, growth 1.3%. Not free: 13 of 100).

Tunisia: (Population 11.5 M, rank 78, growth 1.1%. Free: 78 of 100).

Morocco: (Population 35.7 M, rank 39, growth 1.3%. Partly free: 41 of 100).

South Africa: (Population 56.7 M, rank 25, growth 1.3%. Free, 78 of 100).

Zimbabwe: (Population 16.5 M, rank 70, growth 2.4%. Partly Free, 32 of 100).

Sudan (Population 40.5 M, rank 35, growth 2.4%. Not Free: 6 of 100).

South Sudan (Population 12.5 M, rank 76, growth 2.8%. Not Free: 4 of 100)

Guinea: (Population 12.7 M, rank 75, growth 2.6%. Partly Free, 41 of 100).

Djibouti (Population 957,000, rank 160, growth 1.6%. Not Free: 26 of 100).

Somalia: (Population 14.7 M, rank 74, growth 3%. Not free: 5 of 100).

Niger (Population 21.4 M, rank 57, growth 3.9%. Partly free: 49 of 100).

Nigeria (Population 190.8 M, rank 7, growth 2.6%. Partly free: 50 of 100).

Cameroon (Population 24 M, rank 55, growth 2.6%. Not free: 24 of 100).

Sierra Leone: (Population 7.5 M (rank 103, grows 2.2%). Partly free: 66 of 100)

Chad: (Population 15 M (rank 73, grows 3.1%). Not free: 18 of 100).

The Gambia: (Population 2.1 M (rank 146, grows 3%). Not free: 20 of 100).

Malawi: (Population 18.6 M (rank 61, grows 2.9%). Partly free: 63 of 100).

Rwanda: (Population 12.2 M (rank 77, grows 2.4%). Not free: 24 of 100).

Burkina Faso: (Population 19.1 M (rank 60, grows 2.9%). Partly free: 63 of 100).

Central African Republic: (Population 4.6 M (rank 126, grows 1.4%). Not free: 10 of 100).

Senegal: (Population 15.8 M (rank 72, grows 2.8%). Free: 78 of 100).

Gabon: (Population 2 M (rank 149, grows 2.3%). Partly Free: 32 of 100).

Madagascar: (Population 25.5 M (rank 51, grows 2.7%). Partly Free: 56 of 100).

Democratic Republic of the Congo: (Population 81.3 M (rank 17, grows 3.3%). Not Free: 19 of 100). 26 November 2018. Reports: Congo starts first-ever trial testing of Ebola drugs.

30 November 2018. Reports: The Ebola outbreak in eastern Congo is now the second biggest in history, with 426 confirmed and probable cases, resulting in 245 deaths since Aug. 1. Earlier this week, the WHO launched the first-ever clinical trial for potential Ebola treatments in the country. It includes Gilead's antiviral Remdesivir, and three monoclonal antibody preparations: ZMapp, mAb 114 and Regeneron's 3470-3471-3479.

Angola: (Population 29.7 M (rank 46, grows 3.4%). Not Free: 24 of 100).

Zambia: (Population 17 M (rank 66, grows 3%). Partly Free: 56 of 100).

United Republic of Tanzania: (Population 57 M (rank 24, grows 3.1%). Partly Free: 58 of 100).

Medical

A Madison, WI-based company said its test can identify metabolic subtypes associated with the Autism Spectrum, and can be used to screen children as young as 18 months.

Improved communication skills may be linked to increased connectivity between auditory and motor regions of the brain, researchers at Université de Montreal and McGill University find. Therefore, music improves social communication in autistic children
– Université de Montreal, Translational Psychology, Oct. 23, 2018

Young adults, who are educated about dietary supplements in college, are more likely to use them appropriately, according to new research from Binghamton University, State University at New York. Journal of Dietary Supplements, Sept-2018

FDA approves Udenyca, which is biosimilar to Neulasta.

FDA panel backs Sage Therapeutics' postpartum depression drug Zulresso.

Researchers at University of California San Diego School of Medicine and Kaiser Permanente have discovered that mothers who breastfed a child or children for six months or more are at lower risk for developing non-alcoholic fatty liver disease (NAFLD).
– University of California San Diego Health, Journal of Hepatology

Intuitive Surgical has been dominant in surgical robotics for many years now, but Medtronic and Verb both have systems that are coming, and will be in direct competition with the system da Vinci.

The Bedford, MA-based company NinePoint received approval from FDA for the AI-based IRIS upgrade for the NvisionVLE Imaging System, which is used in the imaging of esophageal tissue.

FDA approves powerful opioid pill as IV painkiller alternative.

Abeona was granted licenses to develop gene therapies for four rare disorders.

Bristol-Myers Squibb and Infinity Pharmaceuticals to evaluate Opdivo in combination with IPI-549 in urothelial cancer.

Amgen and Provention Bio enter development collaboration in celiac disease.

There are some currently available preclinical prostate cancer models, and the advantages and limitations of each model for prostate cancer drug discovery are important. Researchers analyze the spectrum of models needed, as well as their impact on comprehensive oncology and immuno-oncology agent development. Preclinical prostate cancer research is hampered by a lack of predictive models to investigate tumorigenesis, and develop new treatment strategies. Preclinical models are difficult to develop, leaving current drug discovery efforts bottlenecked by the limited number of models truly reflecting the diversity of human disease.

Years of research demonstrate beyond doubt that cancer often runs in families—that is, the risk for being diagnosed with a malignancy is influenced by the genes we inherit from our parents. Prostate cancer is highly heritable, meaning that a man's genetic profile greatly affects his odds of developing the disease. In fact, researchers recently discovered that defects, or mutations, in certain genes, that normally play a maintenance role in the body, increase the risk for metastatic prostate cancer, the variety that's hardest to treat. This research has important implications for men with advanced prostate cancer—and for their families as well.

A major advance in technology, called DNA sequencing, is helping scientists learn more about how genes that are passed from parent to child affect the risk for many different diseases. Genes are segments of DNA, the substance that carries a cell's operating instructions. DNA frequently sustains damage, which can be caused by environmental influences, such as tobacco smoke. DNA can also be damaged by "errors" that occur when cells divide and replicate themselves. Both types of damage can eventually cause mutations, which, in turn, may increase the risk for disease.

Gene defects that occur in germ cells (sperm or egg cells) pass from one generation to the next, and are known as germline, or inherited, mutations. Defects that occur in all other cells after conception are called somatic, or acquired, mutations. Fortunately, our cells also have a variety of genes that can repair DNA; they carry instructions for producing proteins that can fix or undo much genetic damage. However, DNA-repair genes themselves can develop mutations. If that happens, DNA damage may go unrepaired, leading to mutations that promote cancer. Unfortunately, DNA-repair gene mutations can also be inherited.

By age 70, the average man's prostate has doubled in size.

The National Comprehensive Cancer Network (NCCN) has recently issued guidance on when genetic testing may be appropriate.

Alphabet's Healthcare Workshop is kicking off at its Sunnyvale campus, amid the company's growing interest in this area. It will convene employees from life-sciences R&D arm Verily, health-focused AI project Google Brain, anti-aging research division Calico, the Google Fit wearables team, and home automation group Nest. The conference is one of the first times Alphabet has arranged a gathering for its many health groups, which are spread out across the organization.

Patients who seek help for an alcohol use disorder (AUD) may be presented with either of two treatment goals: abstinence, or no heavy-drinking days, which are approved by the Food and Drug Administration for use in testing medications to treat AUD.
– Research Society on Alcoholism
Alcoholism: Clinical and Experimental Research

A combination of the standard-of-care chemotherapy drug known as azacitidine, with nivolumab, an immune checkpoint inhibitor, demonstrated an encouraging response rate and overall survival in patients with relapsed or refractory acute myeloid leukemia. – University of Texas M. D. Anderson Cancer Center

Leukemia

FDA approves Bristol-Myers Squibb's Empliciti Combo.

FDA approves return of popular Primatene Mist Asthma Inhaler.

FDA alerts consumers of voluntary recall of Puriton Eye Relief Drops.

NICE recommends Jazz Pharmaceuticals' Vyxeos for adults with specific types of secondary acute myeloid leukemia.

DNA repair treatment shows early promise for treating cancer.

Gut bacteria treatment shows promise for rare genetic kidney condition.

A biotech company uses metal alloys to reshape fragile bones.

The growing number of shelf-stable foods makes it convenient for people to eat while on the go. It is now possible to obtain dairy products without entering the refrigerated aisle. Fermented milk products contain probiotics that have digestive health benefits. Specialists are looking to preserve bacterial viability in ambient products for extended periods.

Oregon State University, College of Engineering researchers have used nanotechnology to develop a means of installing transistor-based glucose sensors directly onto a catheter attached to a wearable pump. The catheter's integrated electronics transmit blood sugar levels, helping diabetics.

A research team from Massachusetts Eye and Ear describes a newly discovered mechanism in a report published in the Journal of Allergy and Clinical Immunology (JACI). The findings shed new light on our immune systems — and also pave the way for drug treatment. The idea is to use exosomes "swarm" to protect against bacteria inhaled through the nose.

New research released today from the University of South Australia, and University of Exeter in the UK, has found the strongest evidence yet that obesity causes depression, even in the absence of other health problems.
– International Journal of Epidemiology

Drug recalls increased, while medical device recalls decreased in Q3 of 2018.

Open source machine learning tool could help choose cancer drugs.

The increased use of aggressive cleaners and disinfectants to prevent hospital-acquired infections (HAIs) has created an industry-wide problem of cracking in medical equipment housings. Proper material selection can prevent housing failures. When specialists evaluate chemical resistance for daily use in medical equipment housings, they must consider multiple factors, including the material's chemical compatibility under stress.

Hepatitis C drugs cure more than 90% of patients, but can cost more than $50,000 per patient. Findings from a new study could lead to big cost savings. In 50% of patients, the standard 12-week treatment regimen could be shortened. – Loyola University Health System, American Association for the Study of Liver Diseases Annual Meeting

Nearly 18 millions of adults in the United States have hay fever, or allergic rhinitis. It's caused by pollens, weeds, grasses, and molds. Many more have allergic reactions to other things in the environment, like dust mites, dogs, and cats. Nasal allergies affect more Americans every year, according to the American College of Allergy, Asthma & Immunology. Allergies are the sixth-leading cause of chronic illness in the U.S., according to the CDC. And they cost Americans more than $18 billions a year.

Precise Bio is trying to develop bio-manufactured eye-related tissues to treat ophthalmic diseases. The company has already transplanted an added-manufactured corneal graft in animals.

Study suggests diabetes medication improves heart structure.

It is estimated that at least one-third of prescriptions for antibiotics, given in U.S. outpatient settings, are inappropriate. The biggest misuse: antibiotics given for viral respiratory infections, such as colds and flu. Antibiotics can treat only bacterial infections. Overuse of the drugs contributes to the development of antibiotic-resistant bacteria, which cause an estimated 2 millions of illnesses and 23,000 deaths in the U.S. each year.

Merck's Keytruda improves overall survival in esophageal cancer study.

Intracranial hemorrhage detection software receives FDA clearance. Artificial intelligence–powered software prioritizes the assessment of computed tomography cases that may have indications of brain bleed.

A new study by University of Minnesota biomedical engineers shows how they stopped cancer cells from moving and spreading, even when the cells changed their movements. The discovery could have a major impact on millions of people undergoing therapies. – University of Minnesota College of Science and Engineering, Nature Communications, Nov. 20, 2018

The company BTG, which has long produced drugs to treat overdoses and rattlesnake bites, has in recent years focused on interventional medicine - using devices to deliver drugs to affected organs.

RenalytixAI has raised money to help advance tests using AI for early detection of kidney disease, and a test that will help in the accurate management of kidney transplant rejection

A startup spawned from Oxford University is trying to commercialize components of a quantum computing technology that could ultimately improve the downstream end of existing diagnostic devices.

FDA approved the first treatment specifically for patients with rare immune disease.

A study, including health data for more than 500,000 children in the U.S., suggests obesity might be to blame for about a quarter (23 to 27%) of asthma in children who are obese. This could mean about 10% of all kids ages 2 to 17. – Duke Health, Pediatrics

Rush University Medical Center has opened Chicago's first center for airway diseases, a comprehensive program to treat people with interrelated chronic conditions such as sinusitis, allergies, asthma and sleep apnea, which affect millions of people.

Pfizer drug was approved for patients suffering from acute myeloid leukemia.

FDA approves treatment for patients with rare type of immune disease.

Gene therapy to restore vision for people with retinal disease was approved in EU.

FDA warns about severe worsening of multiple sclerosis after stopping Gilenya.

Sterilizing medical devices via ethylene oxide (EO) gas is an effective and common practice within the industry. EO gas is active at a relatively low temperature compared to other methods, such as steam, and it is compatible with plastics, polymers, and many products that are not compatible with other sterilization techniques, such as radiation. However, because of the potentially harmful effects of exposure to EO residue to patients, it is crucial to ensure the levels of EO residue meet the standards defined by ISO 10993-7:2008 by using validated testing methods. There are best practices for demonstrating compliance with that standard, and for demonstrating products sterilized via EO gas are safe for use.

Pfizer issues voluntary nationwide recall of six lots of Thermacare Heatwraps

A Chinese researcher who says he created gene-edited babies crossed what scientists consider a forbidden line.

The most popular YouTube videos on prostate cancer often offer misleading or biased medical information that poses potential health risks to patients, an analysis of the media platform shows. – NYU Langone Health, European Urology

A recent study has identified a new molecular genetic driver of lethal prostate cancer, along with a molecule that could be used to attack it. The findings were made in laboratory mice. If confirmed in humans, they could lead to more effective ways to control. deadly prostate cancer. – Cedars-Sinai, Nature Medicine, Nov-2018

FDA approved an oncology drug that targets a key genetic driver of cancer.

FDA approved first biosimilar for treatment of adult patients with non-Hodgkin's lymphoma.

Astellas Pharma AML treatment received FDA approval.

No one knows what drives people with obsessive-compulsive disorder to do what they do, even when they're aware that they shouldn't do it, and when it interferes with normal life. That lack of understanding means about half can't find effective remedies, and brain studies are necessary. – Michigan Medicine - University of Michigan, Biological Psychiatry

A new option – a combination of a standard drug and the new agent venetoclax – has been granted accelerated approval by the Food and Drug Administration for certain AML patients, after a large, multicenter phase 1 clinical trial showed the combination provided good results for elderly AML.– Dana-Farber Cancer Institute, Blood, Oct-2018

Part of the appeal of frozen yogurt, or soft serve ice cream, is pulling the lever to dispense the dessert into a cone. Whether served in a shop or made at home, these foods take time to make, since the freezing process is not immediate, and batches are churned and cooled to create the appropriate consistency. Therefore, the specialists work to find methods that can achieve rapid freezing of dessert products.

The researchers are working for a non-allergenic, plant-based alternative protein to maintain foam stability and product functionality, as Sodium Caseinate does, after freeze-thawing, and over refrigerated storage for whipped topping products.

Now there are tools, which use step-by-step audio, pictorial, and written instructions, to guide bystanders in emergency situations, to confidently treat bleeding injuries.

The Centers for Disease Control and Prevention (CDC) recently published data that showed reported Legionnaires' disease cases are escalating. Furthermore, data taken during August and September showed 31% of all United States reported cases were in New York State. The increase of cases in New York may be due in part to two factors: aging drinking water infrastructure, and increased testing of patients as a result of recent city and state standards.

Overall, last year's flu vaccine was 36% effective, meaning it lowered the risk for getting sick by about one-third. It was only 25% effective against the H3N2 influenza virus, which caused the most illness. A study in the April issue of *Clinical Infectious Diseases* predicts that this year's flu vaccine will only be 20% effective against the H3N2 virus—but that's still better than no protection.

Researchers produce six antibodies to combat zika virus

FDA approved firdapse for treatment of rare autoimmune disorder.

Emerging micro and nanotechnologies could shape the next generation of implantable drug-delivery systems.

For people with extensive coronary artery disease, bypass surgery may beat stents when it comes to boosting quality of life, according to a study in the *Journal of the American College of Cardiology*.

Italy, Venezia, Libreria and Campanile (left), Torre dell'Orologio, San Theodore Column, Basilica, Palazzo Ducale, Lion of Venice Column (right).

Mathematics, Science & Artificial Intelligence (AI)

A biotech company developed biodegradable antimicrobial paint for ships.

Reports: this unnecessary change of time twice a year is harmful to the health of people, especially for those with medical conditions, children, pregnant women, elderly, and working people. Many people ask to stop this nonsense.

Astrobiology is the study of the origin, evolution, distribution, and future of life in the universe. It is an inherently interdisciplinary field that encompasses astronomy, mathematics, biology, geology, heliophysics, and planetary science.

The mathematics behind machine learning is the essential part, and it enables predictive analyses.

Researchers are working on a smart data visualization technique, to manage and represent the most important metrics and data from online conversations.

Near-eye displays—like those used in augmented (AR), virtual (VR), and mixed (MR) reality devices—project visual objects and information in close proximity to the human eye, sometimes encompassing the user's entire angular field of view. This proximity not only magnifies display projections, but also enhances defects, like non-uniformity, line and pixel defects, poor image clarity, and image positioning issues. To accurately test the quality of displays that are viewed so near to the eye, the measurement technique should take into account the position, limitations, and characteristics of the human eye, especially within the unique viewing environment of an AR/VR headset.

Experts would like to improve the current methods for inspecting large chimneys in power plants. Currently, chimney inspections are executed by specialized personnel working at heights with scaffolding, and taking pictures with high resolution cameras. The experts are looking for alternative ways to remotely inspect chimneys using ready or near ready technology. Near ready is defined as something that could be tested within the next 6 months, and has feasibility already tested.

An important mathematical domain is the Mathematics of Epidemics, which analyses mathematical approaches to studying biology, including ecology and infectious disease.

Specialists are looking for a frequency agile LTE connection, that is a method to operate private LTE cellular systems, using non-owned radio spectrum, on a secondary basis. These private cellular systems would be used to support First Responder emergency events on a temporary basis.

As it works to clear space for next-generation faster networks, the FCC has launched the agency's first high-band 5G spectrum auction. The networks are expected to be at least 100 times faster than current 4G, as well as cut latency, or delays. While millimeter-wave spectrum offers faster speeds, it cannot cover big areas, and will require significant new small cell infrastructure deployments.

SpaceX has tied its own record of 18 rocket launches in a year, using a Falcon 9 to send a Qatari communications satellite into space (with its signature booster landing). Four more launches are scheduled in the last six weeks of 2018. SpaceX, along with Telesat Canada and two other companies, also got the approval from FCC to roll out almost 12,000 satellites for its Starlink broadband service.

The new submarine cables are fiber optic based, and handle up to nearly 200 Terabits per second. Theses cables connect all the populated continents, and most major islands. They are a critical part of international communications, handling over 95% of all international traffic. They make international business possible, as well as being key to many national defense efforts. Recently there has been a decided up-tick in submarine cable construction, to meet the ever-growing traffic demand. Of late, a major driver of this traffic has been the international clientele of the on-line powerhouses - Google and others - along with some of the major data centers computing companies, such as Amazon.

After nearly three decades of work, Aurora, a Boeing company, unveiled its autonomous ultra-long endurance, Solar-powered high-altitude platform Odysseus. The platform will have a near limitless flight time, thanks to its cutting-edge technology, and the use of Solar cells to power the propulsion system during the day, and a battery system to keep Odysseus aloft during the night.

On Sept. 30, 1968, the first Boeing 747 rolled out of its custom-built assembly plant in Everett, Washington. From the beginning, everything about the plane, once known as the queen of the skies, was big.

Embedded hardware technology is the sure cure for counterfeiting. Anti-counterfeiting poses a challenge for medical equipment OEMs but his new technology is a good problem solver.

Three clinical trial participants with paralysis chatted with family and friends, shopped online, and controlled tablet computer applications, all by just thinking about pointing and clicking a pointing device, using brain-computer interface.

There are companies that use artificial intelligence for nutrition-related services.

New truly mobile workstations are designed specifically for pharmaceutical, cleanroom, emergency and other demanding users. Compact heavy-duty battery power and wireless connectivity enable full workstation functionality while in motion, saving time and cost in critical pharmaceutical, emergency, and other operations.

AWS has launched an AI microchip aimed at machine learning, called Inferentia, which will offer "high throughput, and low latency inference performance at an extremely low cost."

Insisting on artificial intelligence, Qualcomm has set up a $100 M fund that will invest in startups working in autonomous cars, robotics, and machine learning platforms. The fund, Qualcomm Ventures AI Fund, has already made its first investment in AnyVision, a facial recognition company. The move places Qualcomm against chip industry contemporaries like Intel, Micron, and Nvidia in investing in AI.

A Berkeley Lab-led team (FIONA) has directly measured the mass numbers of two superheavy elements: moscovium (element 115), and nihonium (element 113). – Lawrence Berkeley National Laboratory, Physical Review Letters, Nov. 28, 2018

The ability to combine mathematics, artificial intelligence (AI) technologies, data science, and traditional bioinformatics approaches, presents an opportunity to change drug discovery, by generating models that are more effective in predicting drug-related toxicity, compared to current methodologies. To harness the power of emerging computational biology approaches, and public repositories, researchers are working to identify new and innovative methodologies that help predict drug-induced cardiac pathology, and its translation, from data generated in a real-life case study.

No matter if it's grandma's cookies or commercially produced rolls, pastry lovers expect their baked goods to have a certain "golden brown" allure — but only after baking. A white dough that changes hue during storage, however, can negatively affect that "golden brown" allure. Researchers discovered that white wine and lemon juice combination prevents unwanted discoloration of pastry dough. – American Chemical Society (ACS) Journal of Agricultural and Food Chemistry

Hazelnuts, like olive oil, cheese and other agricultural products, differ in flavor depending on their geographic origin. Because consumers and processors are willing to pay more for better nuts — especially in fine chocolates and other delicacies – specialists are working on authenticating the geographic origin of hazelnuts. – American Chemical Society (ACS)

Journal of Agricultural and Food Chemistry

New research shows wild bees are essential for larger and better blueberry yields – with plumper, faster-ripening berries. The study is the first to show that wild bees improve not only blueberry quantity, but also quality. – University of Vermont
Agriculture, Ecosystems and Environment

AIOps is an emerging technology that combines the usage of artificial intelligence (AI) with operations (Ops), to help solve critical issues that can bring improve business.

General news and issues

Amazon is in late-stage negotiations with Dallas, New York, the Crystal City area of northern Virginia, and a few other candidates, for the location of its second headquarters, WSJ reports. Talks with the leading contenders are in slightly different phases, centering on incentives and real estate. Amazon's HQ2 would bring as many as 50 K jobs, and more than $5 B in investments over nearly two decades

Piling pressure on Walmart and Target, Amazon is also offering free shipping with no purchase minimum, for the first time, this holiday season. The U.S.-only promotion waives the $25 minimum needed for customers outside the Prime loyalty club. The deal lasts until Amazon can no longer promise items in time for Christmas, which typically takes five to eight business days.

There is now a world of endless innovation, rapid application delivery, astonishing user experiences, and the ability to develop almost anything.

More reports surrounding Amazon's second headquarters suggest it may be split evenly between two cities. The motivation is recruiting enough tech talent, and easing potential issues with housing, transit, and other factors, when adding tens of thousands of workers to an area. Amazon also revealed plans to hire thousands of seasonal delivery drivers to supplement the USPS, UPS, FedEx and its own delivery partners.

Reports: In the first half of 2018, there were over 2.8 millions of DDoS attacks by cybercriminals on organizations around the world – every 6 seconds a new attack. The cybercriminals are getting more innovative, and the attacks are getting bigger, because nobody arrests the cybercriminals.
Powered by a complex network of connected devices, IoT botnets have been in the headlines for several years. But now, cybercriminals' IoT DDoS attacks have emerged, crippling

enterprise networks with sustained attacks that are very difficult to detect.

Marriott's Starwood guest reservation database was attacked and breached by cybercriminals, potentially exposing information on about 500 M guests.

People ask the authorities to arrest the cybercriminals.

Reports: The commercial space market is predominantly filled with massive contractors - Boeing, Lockheed Martin and SpaceX - but there's a new side to the commercial space sector. Rocket Lab put seven spacecraft in orbit on Saturday, 10 Nov, with its first commercial launch, hoping to be at the forefront of the small satellite industry. Big price point. The company's 17 m tall Electron rocket costs $5.7 M per launch, compared to almost $60 M for SpaceX's 70 m Falcon 9.

14 November 2018. Reports: Amazon has selected New York's Long Island City, and Northern Virginia's Crystal City, as the sites for its second and third headquarters, WSJ reports, with an announcement expected as soon as today. Other cities may also receive major sites, according to sources. Amazon began the search across North America in September 2017, saying its new HQ2 location (which will now likely be split) would house roughly 50K jobs, and represent billions in investments.

Reports: Amazon has more than 10,000 employees working on its Alexa virtual assistant, and the Echo devices it powers, double the staff in that division a little more than a year ago. The comments came from Dave Limp, SVP of Amazon Devices, at the WSJ Tech D.Live conference. According to Loup Ventures, Amazon has sold an estimated 47 M+ devices in the Echo family since its launch in late 2014, giving it a roughly 51% share of the smart-speaker market.

Reports: At a meeting of Amazon last Thursday, 15 Nov, in Seattle: "Amazon is not too big to fail," Jeff Bezos told the employees. "In fact, I predict one day Amazon will fail. Amazon will go bankrupt. If you look at large companies, their lifespans tend to be 30-plus years, not a hundred-plus years." "If we start to focus on ourselves, instead of focusing on our customers, that will be the beginning of the end," he added. "We have to try and delay that day for as long as possible."

Reports: Amazon's Jeff Bezos has tapped Wei Gao as his technical adviser - a shadow role that accompanies the CEO to all his meetings. Gao was most recently a VP of forecasting, but has held various positions in 13 years at the company. Past holders of technical adviser have generally gone on to key posts at Amazon, including AWS CEO Andy Jassy, Prime Video VP Greg Hart, and Amazon Go VP Dilip Kumar.

Reports: Amazon has joined the bidding for the 22 regional sports networks that Disney is divesting as part of its $71 B purchase of media assets from Fox, CNBC reports. That includes the YES Network, where Amazon is joining Blackstone, a sovereign wealth fund, and the New York Yankees in the bidding. Apollo Global, KKR, Sinclair and Tegna also made first-round bids for the full slate of networks.

Reports: There many complaints against abusers of phone spam. One of the worst offenders is the security company Protect America, which calls 2-3 times per day each person, to annoy them. People ask the government to stop these abusers.

Reports: Amazon's HQ2 search did the rest of the CEOs in America—and their counterparts in state and local government—a huge service. That's right, we should all be thanking Jeff Bezos.

Reports: AWS is launching a satellite connection service, marking Amazon's first public move into space-related hardware. Amazon is further expanding its footprint into health, reportedly starting to sell software that mines patient medical records. A pilot program for Alexa for Business is also said to be waited at WeWork, though it's grown quite popular at Amazon itself.

Russian and international engineers and researchers discussed digital manufacturing at 2018 Global Smart Industry

Conference held November 13th-15th at South Ural State University (SUSU), reports the university press service to RIA Novosti.

Last year, Amazon shipped more than 5 billions of items to Prime members.

Venezia in 2012: Piazza San Marco, with Basilica San Marco (center), Palazzo Ducale (right), Torre dell'Orologgio (left, 1499).

Humor

Benjamin Franklin (January 17, 1706 – April 17, 1790, aged 84 years and 3 months), was an American polymath, and one of the Founding Fathers of the United States. Franklin was a leading author, printer, political theorist, politician, freemason, postmaster, scientist, inventor, humorist, civic activist, statesman, and diplomat. As a scientist he is known for his discoveries and theories regarding electricity. As an inventor, he is known for the lightning rod, bifocals, and the Franklin stove, among other inventions. He founded many civic organizations, including Philadelphia's fire department and the University of Pennsylvania.

"Who is wise? He that learns from everyone.
Who is powerful? He that governs his passions.
Who is rich? He that is content.
Who is that? Nobody."

Universe Axioms
Formulated by Michael M. Dediu

The following axioms are not independent of each other. They express in different ways the same concept of infinity.

Axiom 1. Pointing a theoretical laser from Earth, in any direction, at any time, after a finite amount of time the laser beam will touch an astronomic body.

Axiom 2. In any direction in space starting from Earth, at any time, there is an astronomic body from which the Earth can be theoretically seen.

Axiom 3. Infinity of space: Any straight line passing through the Earth's center intersects an infinite number of astronomic bodies.

Axiom 4. Infinity of time: Representing the time on a line, with the origin at the beginning of the year 1, the time goes to infinite in both positive and negative directions.

Axiom 5. Infinity of life: Because of the infinity of space and time, it is normal to consider that the life exists at any time, in an infinite number of places. Therefore right now, when you are reading this book, there is life outside the Earth, in an infinite number of places, but we do not know yet how to contact them.

Axiom 6. The Earth rotates itself around its polar axis, the Moon and many artificial satellites rotate around the Earth, in the Solar System all the planets and many other objects rotate around the Sun, the Solar System itself rotates around the center of the Milky Way galaxy, the Milky Way galaxy and all the billions of galaxies in our

Universe (denoted U_1) rotate around the center of our Universe U_1, our Universe U_1, together with billions of other similar Universes, are inside a bigger Universe U_2 and rotate around the center of U_2, then U_2 and many others like it are inside a bigger U_3 and rotate around the center of U_3, and so on. Therefore, in general, the Universe U_n together with many similar Universes are inside the bigger Universe U_{n+1} and rotate around the center of U_{n+1}, for any n natural number, which goes to infinity. This can be written in the formula:

$$U_1 \subset U_2 \subset U_3 \subset \ldots \subset U_n \subset U_{n+1} \subset \ldots, \text{ n natural number.}$$

UK, Oxford, Oriel College (1326, in the east range of First quadrangle, the ornate portico in the center, with the inscription Regnante Carolo).

Time Axioms

Formulated by Michael M. Dediu

Axiom 1. Time is the most important force in the Univers.

Axiom 2. Everything is a function of time.

Axiom 3. Time exists in absolutely everything.

Axiom 4. Time creates and distroys everything.

Axiom 5. Time is invisible, inodor, insipid, unpalpabil, unaudible, but exists evrywhere.

Axiom 6. There are infinitezimal time particles, without mass, which are present everywhere, and which actually continuously transform everything.

UK, Cambridge, From Trinity Lane looking south to the west part of the northern façade and entrance of King's College Chapel (1446).

Bibliography

"The Histories" by Polybius
"Discours de la Méthode" by René Descartes
"Meditationes de prima philosophia" by René Descartes
"Philosophiae Naturalis Principia Mathematica" by Isaac Newton
Chinese encyclopedia Gujin Tushu Jicheng (Imperial Encyclopedia)
"Encyclopédie" by Jean-Baptiste le Rond d'Alembert and Denis Diderot
"Encyclopaedia Britannica" by over 4,400 contributors
"Encyclopedia Americana" by Francis Lieber

Michael M. Dediu is also the author of these books (which can be found on Amazon.com, and www.derc.com):

1. Aphorisms and quotations – with examples and explanations
2. Axioms, aphorisms and quotations – with examples and explanations
3. 100 Great Personalities and their Quotations
4. Professor Petre P. Teodorescu – A Great Mathematician and Engineer
5. Professor Ioan Goia – A Dedicated Engineering Professor
6. Venice (Venezia) – a new perspective. A short presentation with photographs
7. La Serenissima (Venice) - a new photographic perspective. A short presentation with many photos
8. Grand Canal – Venice. A new photographic viewpoint. A short presentation with many photos
9. Piazza San Marco – Venice. A different photographic view. A short presentation with many photos
10. Roma (Rome) - La Città Eterna. A new photographic view. A short presentation with many photos
11. Why is Rome so Fascinating? A short presentation with many photos
12. Rome, Boston and Helsinki. A short photographic presentation
13. Rome and Tokyo – two captivating cities. A short photographic presentation
14. Beautiful Places on Earth – A new photographic presentation

15. From Niagara Falls to Mount Fuji via Rome - A novel photographic presentation

16. From the USA and Canada to Italy and Japan - A fresh photographic presentation

17. Paris – Why So Many Call This City Mon Amour - A lovely photographic presentation

18. The City of Light – Paris (La Ville-Lumière) - A kaleidoscopic photographic presentation

19. Paris (Lutetia Parisiorum) – the romance capital of the world - A kaleidoscopic photographic view

20. Paris and Tokyo – a joyful photographic presentation. With a preamble about the Universe

21. From USA to Japan via Canada – A cheerful photographic documentary

22. 200 Wonderful Places, In The Last 50 Years – A personal photographic documentary

23. Must see places in USA and Japan - A kaleidoscopic photographic documentary

24. Grandeurs of the World - A kaleidoscopic photographic documentary

25. Corneliu Leu – writer on the same wavelength as Mark Twain. An American viewpoint

26. From Berkeley to Pompeii via Rome – A kaleidoscopic photographic documentary

27. From America to Europe via Japan - A kaleidoscopic photographic documentary

28. Discover America and Japan - A photographic documentary

29. J. R. Lucas – philosopher on a creative parallel with Plato, An American viewpoint

30. From America to Switzerland via France - A photographic documentary

31. From Bretton Woods to New York via Cape Cod - A photographic documentary

32. Splendid Places on the Atlantic Coast of the U. S. A. - A photographic documentary

33. Fourteen nice Cities on three Continents - A photographic documentary

34. 17 Picturesque Cities on the World Map - A photographic documentary

35. Unforgettable Places from Four Continents, including Trump buildings - A photographic documentary

36. Dediu Newsletter, Volume 1, Number 1, 6 December 2016 – Monthly news, review, comments and suggestions for a better and wiser world

37. Dediu Newsletter, Volume 1, Number 2, 6 January 2017 (available also at www.derc.com).

38. Dediu Newsletter, Volume 1, Number 3, 6 February 2017 (available at www.derc.com).

39. London and Greenwich, - A photographic documentary

40. Dediu Newsletter, Volume 1, Number 4, 6 March 2017 (available also at www.derc.com).

41. Dediu Newsletter, Volume 1, Number 5, 6 April 2017 (available also at www.derc.com).

42. Dediu Newsletter, Volume 1, Number 6, 6 May 2017 (available also at www.derc.com).

43. Dediu Newsletter, Volume 1, Number 7, 6 June 2017 (available also at www.derc.com).

44. London, Oxford and Cambridge, A photographic documentary

45. Dediu Newsletter, Volume 1, Number 8, 6 July 2017 (available also at www.derc.com).

46. Dediu Newsletter, Volume 1, Number 9, 6 August 2017 (available also at www.derc.com).

47. Dediu Newsletter, Volume 1, Number 10, 6 September 2017 (available also at www.derc.com).

48. Three Great Professors: President Woodrow Wilson, Historian German Arciniegas, and Mathematician Gheorghe Vranceanu – A chronological and photographic documentary

49. Dediu Newsletter, Volume 1, Number 11, 6 October 2017 (available also at www.derc.com).

50. Dediu Newsletter, Volume 1, Number 12, 6 November 2017 (available also at www.derc.com).

51. Dediu Newsletter, Volume 2, Number 1 (13), 6 December 2017 (available also at www.derc.com).

52. Two Great Leaders: Augustus and George Washington - A chronological and photographic documentary

53. Dediu Newsletter, Volume 2, Number 2 (14), 6 January 2018 (available also at www.derc.com).

54. Newton, Benjamin Franklin, and Gauss, A chronological and photographic documentary
55. Dediu Newsletter, Volume 2, Number 3 (15), 6 February 2018 (available also at www.derc.com).
56. 2017: World Top Events, But Many Little Known, A chronological and photographic documentary
57. Dediu Newsletter, Volume 2, Number 4 (16), 6 March 2018 (available also at www.derc.com).
58. Vergilius, Horatius, Ovidius, and Shakespeare - A chronological and photographic documentary.
59. Dediu Newsletter, Volume 2, Number 5 (17), 6 April 2018 (available also at www.derc.com).
60. Dediu Newsletter, Volume 2, Number 6 (18), 6 May 2018 (available also at www.derc.com).
61. Vivaldi, Bach, Mozart, and Verdi - A chronological and photographic documentary.
62. Dediu Newsletter, Volume 2, Number 7 (19), 6 June 2018 (available also at www.derc.com).
63. Dediu Newsletter, Volume 2, Number 8 (20), 6 July 2018 (available also at www.derc.com).
64. Dediu Newsletter, Volume 2, Number 9 (21), 6 August 2018 (available also at www.derc.com).
65. World History, a new perspective - A chronological and photographic documentary.
66. World Humor History with over 100 Jokes, a new perspective - A chronological and photographic documentary
67. Dediu Newsletter, Volume 2, Number 10 (22), 6 September 2018 (available also at www.derc.com).
68. Dediu Newsletter, Volume 2, Number 11 (23), 6 October 2018 (available also at www.derc.com).
69. Dediu Newsletter, Volume 2, Number 12 (24), 6 November 2018
70. Da Vinci, Michelangelo, Rembrandt, Rodin - A chronological and photographic documentary

Mathematical research papers published in international mathematical journals

1. Dediu, M. On the lens spaces. *Rev. Roumaine Math. Pures Appl.* **14** (1969) 623-627.

2. Dediu, M. Sur quelques propriétés des espaces lenticulaires. (French) *Rev. Roumaine Math. Pures Appl.* **17** (1972), 871-874.

3. Vranceanu, G; Dediu, M. Tangent vector fields in projective spaces V_3 and in the lens spaces $L^3(3)$. (Romanian) Stud. Cerc. Mat. **24** (1972), 1585-1600.

4. Dediu, M. Tangent vector fields on lens spaces of dimension three (Italian) *Atti Accad. Naz. Lincei Rend. Cl. Sci. Fis. Mat. Natur.* **54** (1974), no. 2, 329-334 (1977

5. Dediu, M. Campi di vettori tangenti sullo spazio lenticolare $L^7(3)$. (Italian) *Atti Accad. Naz. Lincei Rend. Cl. Sci. Fis. Mat. Natur. (8)* **58** (1975), no. 1, 14-17.

6. Dediu, M. Tre campi di vettori tangenti indepedenti sugli spazi lenticolari di dimensione $4n+3$. (Italian) *Atti Accad. Naz. Lincei Rend. Cl. Sci. Fis. Mat. Natur. (8)* **58** (1975), no. 2, 174-178.

7. Dediu, M. Sopra la metrica Vranceanu generalizzata (Italian) *Atti Accad. Naz. Lincei Rend. Cl. Sci. Fis. Mat. Natur. (8)* **58** (1975), no.3, 354-359).

8. Dediu, M. Sopra la metrica Vranceanu generalizzata (Italian) *Atti Accad. Naz. Lincei Rend. Cl. Sci. Fis. Mat. Natur. (8)* **58** (1975), no.3, 354-359).

9. Dediu, S.; Dediu, M. Sopra gli spazi proiettivi. *Rend. Sem. Fac. Sci. Univ. Cagliari* **46** (1976), suppl., 149-152.

10. Dediu, M.; Caddeo, Renzo; Dediu Sofia Alcune proprietà di una superficie immersa in uno spazio di Hilbert. (Italian) *Rend. Ist. Mat. Univ. Trieste* **8** (1976), no. 2, 147-161 (1977)

11. Dediu, S.; Dediu, M.; Caddeo, R. Alcune proprietà della metrica di Vranceanu generalizzata. (Italian) *Rend Sem. Fac. Sci. Univ Cagliari* **46** (1976), suppl., 153-161.

12. Dediu, Sofia; Dediu, M.; Caddeo, Renzo The Vrănceanu metric in local coordinates. (Italian) *Atti Accad. Sci. Lett. Arti Palermo Parte I (4)* **37** (1977/78). 331-339 (1980)

13. Dediu, M.; Caddeo, Renzo; Dediu, Sofia The extension of an *E*-premanifold to an *E*-manifold. (Italian) *Rend. Circ. Mat. Palermo (2)* **27** (1978), no. 3, 353-358.

Japan: the northern side of Kawaguchiko (Lake Kawaguchi, 6 km², 830 m elevation), with a splendid statue (left), 17 km north of Mt. Fuji (3,776 m, 1707 last eruption), 100 km south-west of Tokyo.

Michael M. Dediu is the editor of these books (also on Amazon.com, and www.derc.com):

1. Sophia Dediu: The life and its torrents – Ana. In Europe around 1920
2. Proceedings of the 4th International Conference "Advanced Composite Materials Engineering" COMAT 2012
3. Adolf Shvedchikov: I am an eternal child of spring – poems in English, Italian, French, German, Spanish and Russian
4. Adolf Shvedchikov: Life's Enigma – poems in English, Italian and Russian
5. Adolf Shvedchikov: Everyone wants to be HAPPY – poems in English, Spanish and Russian
6. Adolf Shvedchikov: My Life, My Love – poems in English, Italian and Russian
7. Adolf Shvedchikov: I am the gardener of love – poems in English and Russian
8. Adolf Shvedchikov: Amaretta di Saronno – poems in English and Russian
9. Adolf Shvedchikov: A Russian Rediscovers America
10. Adolf Shvedchikov: Parade of Life - poems in English and Russian
11. Adolf Shvedchikov: Overcoming Sorrow - poems in English and Russian
12. Sophia Dediu: Sophia meets Japan
13. Corneliu Leu: Roosevelt, Churchill, Stalin and Hitler: Their surprising role in Eastern Europe in 1944
14. Proceedings of the 5th International Conference "Computational Mechanics and Virtual Engineering" COMEC 2013
15. Georgeta Simion – Potanga: Beyond Imagination: A Thought-provoking novel inspired from mid-20th century events
16. Ana Dediu: The poetry of my life in Europe and The USA
17. Ana Dediu: The Four Graces
18. Proceedings of the 5th International Conference "Advanced Composite Materials Engineering" COMAT 2014
19. Sophia Dediu: Chocolate Cook Book: Is there such a thing as too much chocolate?

20. Sorin Vlase: Mechanical Identifiability in Automotive Engineering

21. Gabriel Dima: The Evolution of the Aerostructures – Concept and Technologies

22. Proceedings of the 6th International Conference "Computational Mechanics and Virtual Engineering" COMEC 2015

23. Sophia Dediu: Cook Book 1 A-B-C Common sense cooking

24. Sophia Dediu: Dim Sum Spring Festival

25. Ana Dediu and Sophia Dediu: Europe in 1985: A chronological and photographic documentary

Japan: the north side of Mount Fuji (3,776 m, 1707 last eruption), from Kawaguchiko (Lake Kawaguchi, 6 km², 830 m elevation), 100 km south-west of Tokyo, 17 km north of Mt Fuji

www.ingramcontent.com/pod-product-compliance
Lightning Source LLC
Chambersburg PA
CBHW041714200326
41519CB00001B/159